AF316708

THE WRIGHT BROTHERS FOUND THE SECRET TO FLIGHT

Biography of Famous People Grade 3

Children's Biography Books

Orville and Wilbur Wright were successful in making the first human flight using an aircraft that was heavier than air and powered with an engine. This was an amazing milestone which proved to impact transportation around the world.

Even though it took time to perfect, we are now able to travel long distances in shorter times. In today's world, trips that previously would take months by train and boat, can now successfully be traveled in just a few hours by plane. Read further to learn what lead to this discovery.

Modern aircraft

Wilbur Wright

THE EARLY YEARS

Wilbur Wright was born April 16, 1867 in Millville, Indiana, and was about 4 years older than Orville. Orville Wright was born August 19, 1871 in Dayton, Ohio. They were raised in both Ohio and Indiana, traveling between the two states with their family. There were 5 additional siblings.

The two brothers were inseparable until the death in 1912 of Wilbur. Their personalities complemented each other perfectly, as each one provided what the other one lacked. While Orville had lots of enthusiasm and ideas, Wilbur was more mature with his judgments, steady in his habits, and more likely to see the project to its end.

Wright Brothers

Kite

The boys grew up enjoying to invent things. They became interested in flying once their dad gave them a toy helicopter that would fly with the assistance of rubber bands. They proceeded to experiment by making helicopters themselves, and Orville enjoying building kites as well.

During his high school years, Wilbur had intended to attend Yale to study and become a clergyman. Unfortunately, during a hockey game he suffered an injury to his face, preventing him from continuing on with his education. During the next 3 years, he informally continued with his education by reading in his father's massive library.

Wright Brothers

During these early years, Orville and Wilbur helped their father, who was the editor of a journal named the Religious Telescope. They later started their own paper, called West Side News. They proceeded to go into a printing business together producing anything from commercial fliers to religious handouts.

They opened a store called the Wright Cycle Shop in 1892, located in Dayton, Ohio. This became the best occupation for them since it involved the bicycle, one of the most exciting mechanical devices of the era. Once they decided to start investigating problems with their idea of flight, they now had a solid grounding with practical mechanics.

Wright Brothers Bicycle Shop

Otto Lilienthal

The two brothers became interested in gliding experiments after the death of the famous aeronautical Otto Lilienthal. It was at this time that they decided to learn flying theory.

THE IDEA OF FLIGHT

They started their education of flight at a good time since some fundamental theories of aerodynamics had already been discovered, some experimental data was already in existence and more importantly, the internal combustion engine that had recently been discovered was now available as a source of power for their manned flight.

Wright glider

They began mastering and accumulating important information, tested and designed their gliders and models, built their engine and once the data they had obtained was found to be inadequate, they proceeded to conduct their own experiments, that were more thorough.

The Wrights had decided that any previous attempts at flying were not successful since the plans of the early planes required that the pilots move their bodies in order to control the airplane. They felt that it would be a much better plan to be able to control the airplane by wing movement.

Kitty Hawk

They continued flying gliders and double-winged kits to get experience and test their data. They consulted with the U.S. Weather Bureau and decided on an area with sand dunes which was near a small town named Kitty Hawk, North Carolina, for the location of their experiments. It was here they set up camp in September of 1900.

Their first device was not successful in flying as a kite since it was not able to develop an upward force, otherwise known as sufficient lift. They decided instead to fly it as a free glider. They maintained concise records of the successes as well as their failures. Their data conclusively indicated that the information they had was very inaccurate.

Wright brothers wind tunnel

In 1901 they returned to Dayton and built a tunnel where they could control the wind flow to determine what effect it would have on an object (wind tunnel), which was the first tunnel built in the United States. They continued testing more than two hundred models of wing surfaces so as to measure the drag and lift (resistance) factors and testing to find the most suitable designs.

The Brothers also learned that while screw propellers had been used for ships for more than half of a century, there was not any data that was reliable about this subject and there was no theory that allowed them to design the correct propellers. They would have to figure this out mathematically on their own.

Propeller

By this time, not only had they mastered the current body of the science of aeronautics, but they had also added to this science. They went on the build their third glider, using their new findings, and returned to Kitty Hawk during fall of 1902.

After more than a thousand gliding flights, they confirmed their prior data and demonstrated their ability to control the motions of their glider. Since they had learned how to build and control an adequate air frame, they were now determined in applying power to it.

POWER IN FLIGHT

They soon discovered that there were no manufacturers that would take on building the engine meeting their specifications, and they proceeded to build it themselves. They made one with four cylinders and 12 horsepower.

Once it was installed in the frame, it weighed only 750 pounds and was capable of a speed of 31 miles per hour. In the fall of 1903 they took it to Kitty Hawk and made the world's first powered, manned flight in an aircraft that was heavier than air.

Wright brothers plane

This flight, made by Orville, flew 120 feet and lasted 12 seconds. However, on its fourth flight that same day, Wilbur manned the plane and traveled 852 feet in 59 seconds. A gust of wind then damaged the aircraft severely.

They went back to Dayton knowing they were successful and were to build a second machine. They abandoned all of their other activities in 1905 and concentrated solely on aviation development. They obtained the patent for their flying machine on May 22, 1906.

THE IDEAL
VIN FIZ

WHAT'S NEXT FOR THE WRIGHT BROTHERS?

They looked for encouragement from the federal government for their venture and eventually interest became aroused in Washington, D.C. The government had asked for bids for a plane that met certain requirements in 1907. Out of the 22 bids that were received, three were accepted, with only the Wright brothers finishing their contract.

They continued with their experiments in Kitty Hawk, and, in September of 1908, while Wilbur had traveled to France in an attempt at gaining the interest of foreign backers, Orville was successful in demonstrating their contract plane. The government accepted it. However, the event was blemished when a week later, during a crash, a passenger was killed and Orville was injured.

Wright brothers National Memorial

Wright brothers statue

Wilbur's travels to France were proven to be successful for the Wright Brothers. The brothers formed the American Wright Company in 1909, and Wilbur took the lead for directing and setting up this new venture. When he passed away on May 30, 1912, in Dayton, Orville became depressed and felt alone. He sold his rights to the business in 1915 and gave up interest in the manufacturing business so he could return to his experimental work. He did not care for the busy activity of the commercial life.

Orville retired quietly in Dayton, Ohio, and continued to conduct experiments but none of them were proven to be a major discovery. He served on the National Advisory Committee for Aeronautics (this government agency preceded the National Aeronautics and Space Administration). He was a member from 1915 until he died on January 30, 1948 in Dayton.

National Advisory Committee for Aeronautics

Wright Brothers Aviation monument

The Brothers, using their inventiveness, their curiosity, and their unwillingness to give up on their vision, were instrumental in creating a foundation for modern aviation.

OHIO OR NORTH CAROLINA?

Both Ohio and North Carolina take credit for this remarkable invention. Ohio takes credit since they lived there and much of their designing took place while they lived there. North Carolina takes credit since that is where the original flight occurred.

Wright Brothers Memorial
THE FIRST SUCCESSFUL FLIGHT
OF AN AIRPLANE
WAS MADE FROM THIS SPOT BY
ORVILLE WRIGHT
DECEMBER 17, 1903 IN A MACHINE DESIGNED AND BUILT BY
WILBUR WRIGHT AND ORVILLE WRIGHT
THIS TABLET WAS ERECTED BY THE
NATIONAL AERONAUTIC ASSOCIATION
OF THE U.S. SEPTEMBER 17, 1928
TO COMMEMORATE THE TWENTY-FIFTH
ANNIVERSARY OF THIS EVENT

A lot of time, work, and determination went into the discovery of flight. When you hear the roar of plane overhead, or see one flying overhead, think about the amount of work the Wright Brothers put into the creation of the airplane and how far we have come from that first flight in Kitty Hawk.

For more information on the Wright Brothers and the first flight go to your local library, research the internet, and ask questions of your teachers, family and friends.

Visit
BABY PROFESSOR
EDUCATION KIDS
www.BabyProfessorBooks.com
to download Free Baby Professor eBooks
and view our catalog of new and exciting
Children's Books